Hurry Home
Where You Belong

Hurry Home
Where You Belong

OSWALD C. J. HOFFMANN

Concordia Publishing House

St. Louis   London

Concordia Publishing House, St. Louis, Missouri
Concordia Publishing House Ltd., London, E. C. 1
Copyright © 1970 Concordia Publishing House
Library of Congress Catalog Card No. 76-113868

MANUFACTURED IN THE UNITED STATES OF AMERICA

Preface

Jet age. Age of speed. Whatever you name it, our age is a time of hurry. We like to see things move. We equate speed with success. We hurry everything along.

Hurry by itself is no answer to anything. It's like the man in a hurry who jumped into a New York taxi. "Hurry driver. Drive as fast as you can." The driver waited a few minutes. "Why don't you go, driver? I'm in a hurry." "Well," said the hackie, "I'll hurry when you tell me where you want to go."

It's part of our problem today. We are in a hurry all right, in a hurry to get away. We may think we are in a hurry to achieve some goal. All along our hurry may be away from home, away from our true selves, away from God, away from the real goal and end of life.

We hurry away from home to find our own version of freedom—only to find we cannot live with ourselves.

In the big hurry to get away we run into the suffering that interrupts life's dreams or its pleasures.

A man in a hurry to get away from it all has

no time to see trouble as anything but a calamity. Who ever heard of making friends with trouble!

Slowdown in the big hurry brings on the blues. We feel altogether alone, alienated from every other human being. Nerves are jittery and on edge. We worry ourselves sick.

The fury of hurry distorts the value of wholesome fear, turning what is normal and healthy into panic and frenzy. At the end of the street called hurry there is little or nothing to live for.

What's the problem? When hurry takes us far from home, far from a living relationship with God our Father, we have problems. Big problems. Tough problems.

Hurry in another direction. Hurry home where you belong, to the warm circle of God's family, sure of His forgiveness, His power, His guidance.

Home is not only a distant heaven beyond the grave. It is that, make no mistake about it.

Home is wherever you come to meet God, to know God in Jesus Christ, to belong to God by your faith in Christ. God offers Himself to you in the Good News of Christ, crucified and risen again. Learning to trust in Christ by the power of God's Holy Spirit, people like us come home where we belong.

These chapters are about human needs, the feelings and questions and problems that bother us all sometimes and some of us all the time. They are your problems and mine.

The book is more than a description of human

problems. It is meant to help you find power to go on with joy in Christ. Read. Believe. Receive.

Hurry home where you belong.

Contents

Preface   5
  1 What's Your Hurry?   11
  2 Living with Yourself   19
  3 How to Take Suffering   28
  4 Making Friends with Trouble   35
  5 God's Cure for the Blues   47
  6 Never Alone   56
  7 No Reason to Worry   64
  8 A Case of Nerves   72
  9 A Wholesome Fear   81
 10 Nothing to Live For   89

1

What's Your Hurry?

We live in a fast age. Everyone seems to be in a hurry. Everything takes place in a hurry. Newspapers and magazines make hurried mistakes, damaging reputations and tearing down goodwill, under the bland assumption that the pell-mell rush into print justifies their failure to check the accuracy of information or to consider the effect of publishing misinformation.

In a fast age, truth is the loser, along with faith and love and joy and peace and composure. Hurrying through life can rob people of almost everything that makes life worth living. We eat fast, travel fast, work fast, spend money fast, actually convincing ourselves that this is life. We talk ourselves into this purposeless, frenzied rushing around without which many of us would feel uncomfortable. We are the people whose faces the candid camera catches as we emerge from the subway, grimly pursuing the fleeing moment, dashing madly from sales prospect to sales prospect, climbing the ladder of success at the expense of heart failure that is both physical and spiritual.

Are you playing the game of speed? Weaving in and out of traffic, cutting in on others to gain a momentary advantage, trying to beat the lights? Where are you going in such an all-fired hurry? What's your hurry?

"Look carefully how you drive yourselves," said the apostle Paul. He did not say it exactly that way. Men of affairs in his day owned no motor cars, and few rode in chariots. "Look carefully how you walk," urged the apostle, "not as unwise men but as wise, making the most of the time, because the days are evil. Therefore do not be foolish, but understand what the will of the Lord is." (Eph. 5:15-17)

Doctors say that many of us ride too much today. Heart specialists keep warning the tired businessman that he does not walk enough. Vigorous walking helps to tone up the system, they say, making the bodily functions work more efficiently.

Paul was a "heart specialist" too. He was not interested either in giving people a free ride or in calling on them merely to "slow down." "Make the best use of your time," he said, "if you want to be a healthy man with heart, knowing what makes life tick — what it takes to live, to satisfy the deepest needs of your inner being."

Time is a precious gift of limited duration. If the gift is to be used, there is not a minute to lose. Don't press the panic button, however, because so much time has gone by unused. Don't rush senselessly into trying to buy back those priceless minutes. Look carefully how you walk right now, learning to make the most of your time, living not as unwise men but as wise.

St. Paul evidently looked on time pretty much as did that professor of surgery who said to his students in medical school, "No, gentlemen, don't be in a hurry, because there is no time to lose."

Whenever time is valuable and its careful use most urgent, panic stands in the wings, ready to take over. That is why there are laws against shouting "Fire!" in a crowded theater. When time is of the essence, people have to stop and consider. Otherwise hurry easily turns into hysteria, with tragic consequences.

Hysteria brought about by unreasoning hurry is running loose in the world today. Young people, having fallen wildly in love and feeling there is not a moment to lose, throw discretion to the winds and rush headlong into a relationship that often ends in nothing but heartache. Bored with life, they try it all over again with someone else and are bored all over again.

"Look carefully," said St. Paul, "how you walk. . . . Make the most of the time, because the days are evil." Good advice, strangely given! We advise people to make hay while the sun shines and to stay inside in stormy weather. We tell our students departing for college, "Make the most of your time, because these are the *best* years of your lives." Looking at time, not optimistically nor pessimistically but realistically, St. Paul "levels" with us: "Make the most of the time. . . . The days are *evil*."

13

No preacher needs to document the case. Scientists, politicians, historians, and the daily newspapers will do it for him. Asked about a poll which showed that more people are afraid of war today than at any time in this century, a distinguished world figure replied: "They have reason to be concerned, for men have learned how to make great new scientific advances, but they have not learned how to get along with one another. We are living in the most dangerous time in history."

In this most dangerous of all periods in history, with the possibility of devastating total destruction hanging over all men, people continue to live as if they had never heard of God—as if He were dead and His will were of no importance to mankind. Of an age like ours St. Paul wrote to young Timothy: "But understand this, that in the last days there will come times of stress. For men will be lovers of self, lovers of money, proud, arrogant, abusive, disobedient to their parents, ungrateful, unholy, inhuman, implacable, slanderers, profligates, fierce, haters of good, treacherous, reckless, swollen with conceit, lovers of pleasure rather than lovers of God, holding the form of religion but denying the power of it." (2 Tim. 3:1-5)

The catalog sounds as if it had been written this morning about what happened yesterday, instead of centuries ago about what could happen today or tomorrow. It can be substantiated today in almost every courtroom, from the police court of the smallest town to the Court of International Justice. Time is of the essence. The days are evil. "Therefore do not be foolish, but understand what the will of the Lord is."

What is the will of the Lord? Simply put — possibly too simply for some tastes — the will of the Lord is that our world should be all light and life, all purity and peace. This is the world as He intended it to be. That is the way it actually was — but no longer!

The world as we know it is not characterized by light and peace. Made in the image of God, with almost divine powers and insight, man has it in his power to remake the world in his own image. The picture of our world, with all of its relationships remolded by a race in rebellion against its Creator, is not a pretty one. Men are at war with each other and with themselves. Trying to find their way out of a jungle of their own making, they only plunge deeper into the dense undergrowth of moral confusion and chaos that they themselves have manufactured. This is the history of the world, written by our fathers and being rewritten in the same style even now by three billion people across the face of our globe.

It is not the will of the Lord that the world should be what it is, filled with darkness and death instead of light and life, given to envy and strife instead of the plenty and peace that God intended men to have.

The will of the Lord can be known. Cutting

through the jungle growth of world history and human waywardness, the great God Himself appeared in history to reclaim what had been lost and to redeem what had gone wrong. All light and life, purity and peace, the Son of God was born the virgin's Son. He came, not with a display of pomp and power but as the lowly Child lying in the manger of a donkey motel. In a world of sickness and poverty, of filthy streets and broken homes He climbed a bleak hill with a wooden crossbeam on His back. Crucified to death there between two thieves, He found His final resting place nearby in a tomb just completed for burial of a lifeless body like His.

The end was really the beginning. On the third day He issued forth from the tomb, brought to life again by the glory of His Father. In resurrection from the dead, He proclaimed peace and pardon for sins great and small to all men, redeemed by what He had offered in atonement for all that is wrong with our world — His priceless and divine life joined both in death and resurrection to our all too human life.

The will of the Lord is clear. In Christ the heart of God was laid bare. For reasons of His own, God loves. Out of pure love for men who had gone wrong, He gave His only Son. For the sake of His Son, God gives and forgives. In the Son there is life and light.

The great irony of our time is that people are too busy to find out what life is all about and what the will of the Lord is, too busy to let time have any meaning, too busy to think, too busy to listen, too busy to believe even Good News when they hear it, too busy to pray.

A syndicated newspaper columnist was asked, "Is it a bad habit to reflect on the meaning of life?" He replied, "Worse than bad — it is dangerous. There is only one answer to what life means," he said, "and that is activity — solving every day's problems by getting something done."

Following that advice and hurrying down the road without benefit of map or roadmarkers will take you exactly nowhere, except possibly to some trackless wilderness from which you will find your way back only with the greatest difficulty.

When you go on a long trip, you talk about making time. But this makes sense only when you know where you are going and set out in the right direction. Making the most of the time is nonsense without a sense of direction. "Do not be foolish," said the apostle. Don't follow the nonsense road. Make the most of the time. Understand what the will of the Lord is. Trust in Christ the Savior, and belong to Him. Join the great company of the lost who have been found, of the sons who were dead but by His grace and mercy have turned up alive.

What's your hurry? Live a little. In all confidence go to meet your God. Accept His gracious forgiveness. Receive the strengthening and steadying power of His Spirit. If you have to hurry,

hurry home where you belong—in God's family, taking your place there as a son of God by faith in Jesus Christ. Enter the ranks and join the march with all who have come alive in Christ. Live life with a due sense of responsibility, not as those who do not know its meaning and purpose but as those who do. Make the best possible use of time despite all the difficulties of these days. Get rid of the vagueness and hesitation. Grasp what every man can know to be the will of God—the good and gracious God who wants all men to be saved and to come to the knowledge of the truth.

"This is life eternal, to know You, the only true God, and Jesus Christ, whom You have sent."

That's life: to be at home with God, no longer a stranger, a homeless wanderer. Come on home, a member of the family of God by faith in Jesus Christ. Hurry home where you belong.

2

Living with Yourself

Some people have trouble living with others. They seem to have a peculiar facility for building up little irritations into big ones and for keeping a quarrel going once it has started.

People who have trouble living with others have trouble living with themselves. Added to their number are all those respectable citizens who get along tolerably well with their neighbors but still have a rough time with themselves. If the truth were known, people who find it difficult or even impossible to live with themselves might turn out to constitute the majority of the population of the world.

Why is it that in some of the world's great cities there is a steady stream of young people coming in after working hours to pay a large fee for 15 minutes' consultation with a psychiatrist? Young people in this mixed-up world are having trouble living with themselves as they try to find meaning in their lives and regretfully admit their failure.

An extensive study of a prosperous suburban community in the United States shows that a great number of suburbanites, after attaining many of the goals they thought were important, have found life to be unbearable. The difficulty, of course, was with themselves, not with their new homes and cars and boats.

Guilt and anxiety are two words that describe a worldwide epidemic affecting the health of people deep down inside where it counts the most. Indeed, the English-speaking world has turned to the German language for a word to describe the problem. The Germans call it *Angst*. Medical people—not ministers—are using this German word to describe what ails people who fill their reception rooms.

It should not surprise us that many people have trouble living with themselves. As they try to make their way in a world filled with cheating, vice, drunkenness, foul talk, infidelity, delinquency, and family quarrels—themselves tainted and tormented by the ills surrounding them—it is not at all unnatural that people should come to the point where their own hearts condemn them.

People have a pretty clear knowledge of what they are—and what they ought to be. They feel the chasm between what they are and what they sense is expected of them, even though they have no clear knowledge of the God who expects it of them. Their very uncertainty about God only complicates the problem. Wondering whether He is and living as if He isn't, they come to the quite natural conclusion that they themselves are not worth a shot of powder.

At least this may be a step in the right direction. People living without God ought to be troubled. If God made this world of ours and still stands in moral judgment over it, no one is going to arrive at peace of mind by ruling Him out of existence. The remedy lies not in ignoring Him but in facing up to what is—and must remain—a fact of life: There is a God whose judgments are pure and right altogether.

Try to kid yourself into believing that you can simply forget about God, to whom you must give answer for the very things that trouble you. Do everything possible to numb your senses in such a way as to forget that feeling, that gnawing feeling of guilt. Keep yourself so busy that you have no time to think. These methods are being tried all the time, but the world is no better for all the effort being put into them.

When everything has been tried, the truth still comes up sharp and clear: Without God it won't work. Without God life is not complete. Apart from God you are going to have trouble living with yourself.

The apostle John knew God, and he knew troubled hearts. He wasted no time on ineffective solutions. He did not attempt to cajole people out of their anxieties by telling them they were just imagining things. This is what he said: "Hereby we . . . shall assure our hearts before Him. For if our heart condemn us, God is greater than our heart." (1 John 3:19-20)

Do you have trouble living with yourself? Are you worried about the things you think and say and see? If you are, you may not be so different from other people as you imagine. Taking a good hard look at yourself is not necessarily neurotic. It becomes neurotic only when you try to cover up.

I am not an authority on neuroticism, but I can quote a man who is. He is not a Christian, but he is a realist. This eminent psychologist points out that the so-called neurotic is very often a bona fide sinner whose guilt from the past is real, whose difficulties arise not from inhibitions but from actions clearly proscribed socially and morally which he has kept carefully concealed, unconfessed, and unforgiven. That is a psychiatrist talking, not a preacher.

Now let the preacher talk. There is a heart greater than your own. If you have trouble living with yourself, get outside yourself and get in touch with the heart that is greater than your own. That heart belongs to God. It is filled with love for people just like you. It is the heart of One who understands and is ready to help. He knows who you are and what you have done — and still He forgives. He is a Father, bent not on condemning but on redeeming and receiving. Knowing Him makes all the difference in the world.

It would be hard to find anyone who had more trouble living with himself than the young man in the story told by Jesus Christ. You remember the headstrong character who decided his father's house was too narrow for him and went out to make his own way, using the resources of the inheritance he had demanded from his father before he had it coming to him. His father gave him what he wanted, and he went out to sow his wild oats. When he had used up all his money in a far country, he came to himself. He determined to return and even decided what he would say when he met his father: "Father, I have sinned against heaven and before you; I am no longer worthy to be called your son."

When the son returned, there was the father standing on a hill waiting for him. You will recall the joyous scene that resulted as the father embraced him, put a ring on his finger, and called out to the servants: "Bring the fatted calf and kill it, and let us eat and make merry; for this my son was dead and is alive again; he was lost and is found" (Luke 15:24). So the festivities began, conducted by father, son, and servants — all together.

One thing is notable about this young man. He recognized that he had a problem. He really came to himself when he began to see that his problem was living with himself. The trouble with many people today is that they blame others for their troubles. St. John implies that it is not so bad to find ourselves condemned in our own hearts if thereby we find the great heart of God, where we are not condemned.

People instinctively feel that they ought to be condemned by God. They even resent the thought that Christ died for their sins, feeling that they ought to atone for their own sins. They have this feeling because they do not know God. God has a great heart. Out of that great heart He sent His only-begotten Son into the world that whoever believes in Him may not perish but have everlasting life.

Displeasing God is not a trivial matter. A man who says he will pay for his own sins, by that statement shows that he does not take God very seriously. Of course we consider it praiseworthy when a man wants to earn his own way, shoulder his own burden, and pay his own debts. Any man, however, who thinks he *can* pay his debt to God is naive; he is an arrogant man if he thinks he *has* paid that debt.

It is probably just as arrogant to plead, as I have heard some people do, that God could not possibly forgive them. They want to put a halo around their wrongdoing, as if it were beyond God's ability to do anything about it. God has a great heart. He did what many consider unnecessary and others think impossible. He sent His Son to atone for the sins of the world. No one is excluded, and everyone is included in that divine act.

If you have trouble living with yourself and come to recognize that your problem is in yourself, you have taken the first step toward that great heart of God which is wide open to you. Don't try to treat the symptoms; get at the cause.

If your heart condemns you, there is a reason for it. If you hate yourself, you probably know why. Even if you don't know why, God's heart is big enough to take you in, and His arms are strong enough to enfold you.

God forgives and God forgets. If He forgets, why don't you? Don't forget the lesson, but forget the guilt. Christ died to put that guilt away, to sweep it out of the house, to sink it in the great deep where it will never be found. This is the way God's great heart works.

Put that self-condemnation and self-hatred out of your heart. Take to your heart the good God with His great heart. Have confidence that He really wants you to be His own to live with Him in His kingdom. There is good reason for having this confidence. Christ died for you, and He lives for you. He paid the price for you, and His strong hand is ready to take yours along whatever rocky road lies ahead.

"Beloved," said John, "if our heart condemn us not, then have we confidence toward God. And whatsoever we ask, we receive of Him because we keep His commandments and do those things that are pleasing in His sight" (1 John 3:21-22). Confidence in God's great heart begins and builds an entirely new life. New and wonderful things begin to happen when a man puts his confidence in God, when he accepts God's love, His forgiveness, His strength, His life. Confidence in God changes a man's heart and outlook. Our hearts no longer condemn us when we enjoy fellowship with God, leading us to ask and do the right things. As two people in love sense what the other wants and have no trouble doing what the other wants, so fellowship with God leads to an obedience which is pleasing to the great heart of God.

People always have wondered what they could do to please God. They asked that question of Christ: "What must we do to do the will of God?" Christ answered: "His will is to believe on Him whom God hath sent." That's St. John's answer to the same question. "This is His commandment, that we should believe on the name of His Son Jesus Christ and love one another as He gave us commandment." (1 John 3:23)

God's Son walked this earth of ours, lived our kind of life, and went all the way into death. He knew what life is all about. He stretched out His arms, and they nailed His hands to a cross. Out of God's great heart He came, and to God's great heart He has gone in resurrection from the dead. There is no reason to despair. Christ lives!

If your heart condemns you, do not despair. Instead of looking to yourself, look to God. Instead of trusting yourself, trust Christ. If our shriveled little hearts give us small comfort, God's great heart is always there, warming our littleness, brightening our darkness, and transforming death into life.

God's great Son experienced our fears and heartaches, our suffering and death, for one purpose: that we might experience His grace and truth, His forgiveness and life—His love. If our heart condemns us, this is His commandment, that we should believe on the name of His Son Jesus Christ and love one another as He gave us commandment.

Get outside yourself. Turn the spotlight away from your own problems, and focus it on those of others. Reflect the light of God's great heart into those dark corners where people live—where those multitudes live who have trouble getting along with themselves. With confidence in God, your heart assured before Him in the certainty that God's great heart is greater than any problem or pettiness that afflicts you, go along the road of His commandment. Believe in Jesus Christ, and show the consideration of love to those about you.

In an age of secularism people are tempted to say, "Nobody up there loves me, because there is nobody up there." There is still God and His great heart. Knowing the heart of God, believing on the name of His Son Jesus Christ, living lovingly with your neighbor, live happily with yourself.

3

How to Take Suffering

When we are in pain, no one needs to remind us of the reality of suffering. Our problem is how to take it. Even if we are in good health, we have to remember that suffering may strike us too. Sooner or later suffering comes to all of us.

St. Paul instructs us how to take suffering. In one memorable passage he refers to his own personal example. He speaks about "a thorn in the flesh, the messenger of Satan to buffet me, lest I should be exalted above measure.

"For this thing I besought the Lord thrice that it might depart from me. And He said unto me, My grace is sufficient for thee; for My strength is made perfect in weakness. Most gladly therefore will I rather glory in my infirmities that the power of Christ may rest upon me.

"Therefore I take pleasure in infirmities, in reproaches, in necessities, in persecutions, in distresses for Christ's sake; for when I am weak, then am I strong." (2 Cor. 12:7-10)

In one of his three-minute plays Thornton Wilder tells of an infirm physician who stood one day by the pool of Bethesda waiting for the water to be troubled that he might be made whole again.

The angel, whose business it was to trouble the water, came to him and said: "Stand back. Healing is not for you. Without your wound where would your power be that sends your low voice trembling into the hearts of men? We ourselves, the very angels of God in heaven, cannot persuade the wretched and blundering children of earth as can one human being broken on the wheels of living. In love's service only wounded soldiers will do."

Suffering has a purpose — a purpose that God makes clear through personal experience. It would be difficult to find anyone with more experience in hardship and suffering than St. Paul had acquired in his long missionary career. To complicate his life even more, he had what he called a "thorn in the flesh" — very likely a nagging physical disorder. Three times he prayed desperately to the Lord to take this annoyance, this burden, from him — without success. Instead the Lord pointed out a few facts to him, including the value of suffering. He supported Paul and gave Paul the strength to take suffering, to live with it and even to like it.

Paul became content with all kinds of weaknesses and indignities that people without his outlook on life would almost certainly call bad. In fact, he was glad to boast of his infirmities that, as he put it, "the power of Christ may rest upon me."

How does a man arrive at this way of looking at things, this fully developed and mature character which we must admire from afar but hardly dare to dream of possessing ourselves?

First of all, we have to be able to look suffering in the eye. By that I do not mean that any of us can stare it down and browbeat it into submission. We must just see suffering for what it is.

St. Paul calls suffering the messenger of Satan. God did not devise suffering for the human race, nor did He plan that we should writhe on a bed of pain. His plan was that all men should live free of pain and sorrow, untouched by misery and grief. Where did this corruption of life come from, then? It came from the father of evil, to whom our first parents succumbed. We bear the stigmata of that surrender today. When we start laying the blame for the presence of suffering, let's lay it where it belongs. It does not rest on God.

Still God uses suffering for His own purposes, now that it is here, now that we have brought it on ourselves. Everything in the universe is still under control. God's control. God has not been overpowered, and He will let things go only so far. In the lives of those who love Him, God will take the very evil that afflicts them and will turn it into a blessing, both for the sufferers themselves and for others.

None of us seeks out suffering, nor does God want us to do that, lest we put a halo around our misfortunes and feel that they make us good or at least better than others. Each of us can stand some suffering if for no other reason than to expose our weaknesses, to erode our arrogance and self-appreciation.

Paul was a man of strong will and brilliant intellect. He had a good deal of the pride we find in young intellectuals today, especially if they have carved out a niche for themselves through an outstanding academic record or through a meteoric career in their chosen profession.

A certain blindness often develops in those circumstances which makes a man feel that he is it, that he doesn't need other people, that he doesn't need God.

Paul was a little like that even after becoming a Christian and a minister of Jesus Christ. He did not always stop to look at himself, to see himself as he actually was. Then came this problem, this infirmity, this thorn in the flesh. He stopped. He looked. He listened. He heard God talking—not just talking, but talking to him, Paul the self-sufficient. It may have been that Paul was flat on his back when he asked God to be relieved of his difficulty so that he might be free to do what he wanted to do, liberated to do what God wanted him to do.

He discovered that he was not going to get his wish. He was going to have to live with this burden; he was going to have to work with it.

It was a hard lesson, and a great one, for Paul to learn. It is just as hard and great for us to learn today. When we tend to forget God, to depend on ourselves rather than on His mercy, His grace,

31

His love, God will not stop at drastic measures to bring us back to ourselves, to what He wants us to be. A quite incidental result of this process is that a person becomes a much more rounded personality than he formerly was, a more agreeable and likable person, more capable of understanding other people's problems and in a better position to achieve his own objectives in life. These results are quite incidental, though they may be more obvious to our friends and associates than are God's deeper purposes for each one of us.

God's deeper purpose is hidden in His own heart—and in ours. He wants each of us for Himself. He has redeemed us. He does not want that redemption to go uncollected. He has paid the price—the great price of His Son's sacrifice—and He does not want it to be rejected through indifference or oversight. His purpose is not punishment in this case but pardon, the kind He extends to all men.

Have you known suffering? Its purpose was to wring an admission from you in a quiet confessional just between you and God: "God, was I trying to fool You? Forgive me. I can't get along without You. I need You every hour."

God's answer to that kind of confession is: "My grace is sufficient for you. It does the job. I forgive you. I sent My Son that you would not have to suffer for what you have done. He was crucified, He was punished, and you are forgiven. Don't be alarmed, and don't be disturbed by your pain. My grace is sufficient for you. My power is made perfect in weakness."

Christ will deal with our suffering. He will remove it — or He will give the power to bear it. "When I am weak," said St. Paul, "then am I strong. When my own strength is gone, Christ's strength is with me and will bear me up."

Christ has a heart for sufferers. They are His special care. He is particularly generous to them. He supplies courage and patience of the kind they could never muster themselves. He becomes their Lord in a fuller measure, in the sense that He often rules their lives more completely and uses them to influence others more deeply than if they were running around without a care in the world.

How should you take suffering? St. Paul says, "Take it gladly, that the power of Christ may rest upon you." Knowing God's purpose in suffering, and the power of Christ that attends it, makes all the difference in the world.

God's ways are seldom our ways. It might be better to say they are never our ways. In God's hand, suffering becomes a saving bit of surgery, a kind of healing. It still hurts, it is still uncomfortable, but it can be accepted willingly and even cheerfully. It can be the supercharger which God uses to fill your life with new and unexpected power.

How take suffering? Never in the spirit of bitterness. This would be yielding to the evil that originally brought suffering into the world, into your own life. How take suffering? Always in the cheerfulness of faith in Christ, in His redemptive power.

Suffering will come your way now or later. Be confident that it is bringing with it a special present from God to you—the gift of His love and consideration. That gift will be evident to everyone around you, as Alan Porter once said:

Every countenance
That warms and lights the heart of the beholder
Shows, clear and true, the signature of pain.

—*Signature of Pain, and Other Poems* (New York: John Day Co., 1931)

4

Making Friends
with Trouble

How do you meet trouble? Whether you are
sixteen or sixty, living in financial comfort or
just managing to make ends meet, a faithful
churchgoer or never setting foot inside a church,
the question is never hypothetical. All of us have
to be prepared for trouble.

Some are hit harder than others. One may
experience only little pinpricks of trouble; another
will receive wounds that are deep and deadly. One
person will lose his wallet; another will lose his
business. One person suffers a blister; another
suffers a coronary. One man sees his plans for
tomorrow wrecked; another finds his hopes for
a lifetime crushed.

Little or big, troubles will come. It may be in
a doctor's diagnosis or in a teen-ager's tantrum;
through friction at the office or through the pettiness of friends; from a thoughtless spouse or
from a conniving enemy; through the death of
a loved one or through injury sustained at the
hands of a complete stranger.

The question is: How do you meet trouble?

35

It could very well be that you have never thought of that question. You try to avoid trouble and are completely unprepared for it when it comes.

James, a servant of God and of the Lord Jesus Christ, a practical pastor ministering to the needs of ordinary people, talking about what happens every day, addressed himself first of all to this question: How do you meet trouble?

"When all kinds of trials and temptations crowd into your lives, my brothers," he said, "don't resent them as intruders, but welcome them as friends! Realize that they come to test your faith and to produce in you the quality of endurance. But let the process go on until that endurance is fully developed, and you will find you have become men of mature character with the right sort of independence." (James 1:2-4 Phillips)

Speaking to the early Christians in the apostolic church, people who had come to know the Lord Jesus Christ as their personal Savior and yet were going through all kinds of difficulty and trouble, the apostle gave a good piece of advice: Don't resent trials! Welcome them! Make friends with trouble because it can make a lasting contribution to your life. Trouble will do that for you, that is, if you are prepared to meet it in the right way.

The first step in the process of meeting trouble in the right way is to take a good look at yourself. Who are you? What kind of things are important to you? What kind of defense have you built up around yourself in the form of pretense? Who do you think you are, anyway?

This man James was plainspoken. He did not mince words. Apparently he had talked to enough people about their troubles to realize that you can't beat about the bush. "The brother who is poor," he said, "may be glad because God has called him to the true riches. The rich may be glad that God has shown him his spiritual poverty. For the rich man, as such, will wither away as surely as summer flowers. One day the sunrise brings a scorching wind; the grass withers at once, and so do all the flowers—all that lovely sight is destroyed. Just as surely will the rich man and all his extravagant ways fall into the blight of decay." (James 1:9-11 Phillips)

This is tough talk from a pastor who had a real heart for people. He did not believe, however, that he was doing people a favor by telling them life does not hurt. He knew the hurts of life, and what it takes to heal.

This man knew the healing power of faith in Jesus Christ. Faith is no dream—not when it is faith in Jesus Christ. Faith in Christ heals. Christ died and Christ rose again. Christ forgives and Christ gives. In His death and resurrection there is forgiveness and healing for every man. Why pass that up when it is available to everyone? Why cover up, or pretend to be what you are not, when Christ takes you as you are and heals? Why worry about being rich or poor when the true riches come from God's grace and everything is temporary and transient? Why depend on physical vigor or brains or money when they are all destined to go, eventually, like the flowers before the scorching wind, like the grass withering at the end of day, like everything else that is to know the blight of decay? Depend on God, who gives generously to all men, especially that necessary wisdom that comes from knowing Him and Jesus Christ, whom He has sent.

This man James was a real pastor. He knew people. Recognizing how quickly bitter thoughts spring into the human mind and bitter words issue forth from human lips, he addressed himself to the universal problem of trouble. He knew the questions people ask: "Why? Why did this have to happen to me?" He was well aware of the easy way people excuse themselves and accuse everyone else, including God, for their troubles. This is what he had to say about that:

"The man who patiently endures the temptations and trials that come to him is the truly happy man. For once his testing is complete, he will receive the crown of life which the Lord has promised to all who love Him.

"A man must not say when he is tempted, 'God is tempting me.' For God has no dealings with evil and does not Himself tempt anyone. No, a man's temptation is due to the pull of his own inward desires, which can be enormously attractive. His own desire takes hold of him, and that produces sin. And sin in the long run means death — make no mistake about that, brothers of mine! But every good endowment that we possess and every complete gift that we have received must come from above, from the Father of all lights, with whom there is never the slightest variation or shadow of inconsistency. By His own wish He made us His own sons through the Word of truth that we might be, so to speak, the first specimens of His new creation." (James 1:12-18 Phillips)

All of us have a tendency to see others as far less conscientious than we, far less generous, far less religious. Satisfied with ourselves, we roll merrily along the highway of life, enjoying every minute of it, with not a care in the world. All of a sudden, trouble hits. Through clenched teeth we mutter, "Why me?"

Trouble has a way of getting in the way of our well-laid plans. We know what we want. Our goals are clear. We are on our way. All of a sudden, out of the clear, blue sky, along comes misfortune in the form of some problem that throws a monkey wrench into the whole business. This is not the way we planned it at all! Here we are on a four-lane highway, not even thinking about those bumpy, winding, and dangerous side roads. Now we find ourselves on such a side road. How come? It is a good question, especially because most of us have the tendency to absolve ourselves of any responsibility for misfortune. The apostle knew exactly how people react. "Let no one say when he is tempted or tested, 'I am tested and tempted by God.' God cannot be tempted with evil. He Himself tempts no one; the fact is that every person who is tempted is lured and enticed by his own desires. Desire conceives and gives birth to sin; sin, when it is full grown, brings forth death."

In the midst of misfortune it is a common human strategy to shake off reality, to complain, "What a raw deal I've had!" Some people even find grim satisfaction in shaking their fists at God and holding Him responsible.

"Hold on!" says this practical pastor. "If there is evil involved, don't blame God." God does indeed test us. But He does not try to trip men up and make them fall into sin. He sets no traps. When we get enmeshed in evil, it is our own fault and responsibility.

The pull of our own inward desires, the lure of our own lusts, the attraction of our own deluded passions draws us into paths that are wayward because they lead away from God. When desire, lust, and passion produce their customary fruit, we have what the Bible calls sin—transgression in some form or other of God's will and way. When sin is full grown, it produces death. Don't blame God for that! We dig our own graves when we fall into sin. "Do not be deceived, my beloved brethren. Every good endowment and every perfect gift is from above, coming down from the Father of lights, with whom there is no variation or shadow due to change. Of His own will He brought us forth by the Word of truth that we should be a kind of firstfruits of His creatures." (RSV)

When ancient Job was down and out, his wife gave him a perfectly human piece of advice. "Why don't you curse God and die?" she said. You can't win, she was saying. Look where your conscientious life has got you. A fine God you have! He takes delight in making you squirm. Forget Him! Tell Him what you think of Him—and find release, if you can, in death.

Job replied, "You are talking like a foolish woman. Shall I curse God, who has given me so much good, just because evil shows up in my life?" Here was a man, a real man, who could not forget God. He was not trying to smile weakly and ignore evil. He could not forget what had happened to him, with constant pain wracking his body because of disease, with constant worry over the loss of his possessions, with the cutting memory of his children's death still fresh in his mind. Not ignoring the pain, not overlooking the evil, and not blaming God, he went on to live, recognizing that God is not the author of evil. This man knew that if he cursed God, then he would die. That would be the end of everything. As long as there is God, there is always hope. As long as God cares, man can have courage. "Though He slay me, yet will I trust in Him," said Job, tested as few have been tested.

If God seems far away, it is not because He has turned His back on you. You may have turned your back on Him, but He has not turned His back on you. You may resent His intrusion into your life, but He cares and will not turn His back on you. He is the good God on whom you can depend. "Every good endowment you possess and every complete gift you have received comes from Him with whom there is never the slightest variation or shadow of inconsistency."

How can you know that God cares? that He will not turn His back on you? The answer is plain: God the Father sent His eternal and unique Son, Jesus Christ, to be a man just for you. He suffered all the privations of life and all the agony of death just for you. Not for Himself, mind you, but for you. He invites you to have faith in Him. By faith in Christ you become a member of God's family, a true son or daughter, steady in your trust and ready to follow.

You consider yourself to be a Christian. You have some trust in Christ. You are ready, at least at times, to follow Him. Still trouble strikes. What is one to think about that?

The apostle answers: "Don't be surprised. Temptations and trials do come into the lives of the best of Christians. The man who patiently endures temptations and trials that come to him is the truly happy man. For once his testing is complete, he will receive the crown of life which the Lord has promised to all who love Him. Remember this: Of His own will, because He wanted to, God the Father made you His own son through the Word of truth, that is, the Good News in Christ, that you might be, so to speak, a specimen of His new creation."

When temptations and trials come along, a man shows what he is made of. Does he grouse and complain? Or does he meet trouble and testing with the glorious fortitude of faith that turns a time of trouble into a time of triumph?

Trouble convinces every one of us that we are not spectators to the game but active participants on the field where the battle must be fought. You can surrender, of course, to temptation or trial or whatever it is that hits you. You can surrender and go the way of so many people who spend their lives complaining about their lot.

The alternative is to put up a fight. You can put up a fight with God against temptation or trial or what have you and come out on top. The man who does that is blessed. "Blessed is the man," said James, "who endures trial, for when he has stood the test, he will receive the crown of life which God has promised to those who love Him." (RSV)

Victory comes through faith in Christ. Christ knew trouble. He knew all about it. He was a man in every sense of the word. He accepted willingly all the pain and suffering that is common to man, all the trial and temptation to which men are heir. Writers who try to picture Jesus Christ are

43

never faithful to the truth unless they show Him as He was: a man of sorrows and acquainted with grief, in His face the sign of struggle.

This does not mean that Christ went around looking sad. He was the living example of what St. James was talking about: "Count it all joy, my brethren, when you meet various trials." Our Lord knew joy in the midst of struggle. His patience was pushed to the limit. His temper was strained to the breaking point. He knew the treachery of enemies and the betrayal of friends. Kindness was repaid with insults, and love with hatred. He showed the effects of the struggle when He pleaded that the bitter cup might be taken from Him. His Father willed otherwise, however. Tasting the cup to the full, He endured and won through to victory for every man.

How can you meet trouble? By faith in Christ. "This is the victory that overcomes the world, our faith. Who is it that overcomes . . . but he who believes that Jesus is the Son of God?" (1 John 5:4-5)

Enduring with Him, sharing His suffering, any man can taste the joy His Father gives. He rose from the dead, ascended into heaven, and wears the crown of life. Sharing His suffering, you share His glory.

It is His promise to you: You can taste that same joy, wear the same crown! Listen to this word from God: "Blessed is the man who endures trial, for when he has stood the test, he will receive the

44

crown of life which God has promised to those who love Him." This is God's gift to those who make friends with trouble, overcoming by faith in Christ and arriving at a full-blown maturity that knows what it means to make friends with trouble and then to overcome.

Every factory that produces life-preserving drugs and medicines has a laboratory to run constant tests on what is being produced. A terrible tragedy could result if something went wrong with the ingredients or with the mixture, changing the product from something good to something lethal. How much we depend on that testing!

There are all kinds of faith, with all kinds of ingredients, depending on the makeup of people, the experience they have had, their temperament, their success or failure, their intellectual or emotional capacities, and a lot of other things that go to make up a man. Testing and trial help that faith of yours to run firm in the right channel and in the right direction. Trouble and torment are used by God to build real faith — faith in the God who gives not evil but good, who sends us not stones but bread, who offers pardon in the place of punishment, who leads not to tragedy but toward triumph.

You may not always understand His ways, but you can trust Him. Whatever is good in the world comes from Him, and everything that comes from Him is good. He is the one consistent Person in this most inconsistent world of ours.

Nothing else is altogether sure. Scientific premises that we bank on today may be altogether changed ten years from now or even ten days from now. The world our grandchildren will know may be far different from the one you and I know today. Times change, standards change, ways of life change.

But God does not change. It is His nature to give good gifts. He gives His good gifts to you today in Jesus Christ. He will give them to you tomorrow in a world of interplanetary travel and electronic miracles.

What is His gift? In a nutshell, it is forgiveness. Faith in the forgiving love of God produces strength and maturity; faith builds wisdom and character; faith produces endurance. It makes men as God intended men to be.

The Giver of all good things reaches out to you. By the Word of truth, the truth that is in Him and in His Son Jesus Christ, He reaches out to make you His son, His daughter, with faith ready to meet trouble — even to make friends with trouble.

For the joy that was set before Him, our Lord endured the cross, despising the shame, and was set down at the right hand of the Majesty on high. Blessed the man who takes trouble with faith in Christ — makes friends with trouble — and goes on with maturity of character to receive the crown of life which God has promised to those who love Him.

5

God's Cure for the Blues

If the devil were ever to lay out his tools for sale at public auction, one would have special status. The others would be there: envy, jealousy, lust, pride, greed, laziness, and all the rest. One tool, however, would command a price all its own for its power to injure and destroy.

That tool is discouragement. Once the devil is able to plant discouragement into a man's heart, the way is open for almost anything else he wishes to do.

Discouragement is at large in the world. Letters, publications, conversations are full of it.

Where is the man or woman who has not at some time or other had a good case of the blues? The blues take over when faith falters. Faith falters when people say, "We believe in God the Father Almighty," and then act as if God had gone on vacation.

With its temptation to despair of God even as we despair of ourselves, discouragement is often seized upon by God Himself to make us exercise the flabby muscles of faith, forcing us to train for the race of life as athletes go into training for their next test of endurance and strength.

God's way is not easy. Many faithful in every generation have discovered this truth for themselves. Charles Spurgeon, the great English preacher of the last century, preached for over thirty years in London to an average of 5,000 people every Sunday morning and 5,000 people every Sunday evening. Yet, one of his biographers points out, this man of God was frequently in the grip of terrific moods of depression. (Richard E. Day, *The Shadow of the Broad Brim*, p. 173)

You can be God's man or woman and still be subject to the blues. An outstanding example is a great man of God whose experience is described in the 19th chapter of the First Book of Kings. Immediately after the most dramatic and triumphant moment of his life, the conquest of the priests of Baal and the coming of the rains so long withheld, Elijah hurried to anticipate the arrival of King Ahab in the city of Jezreel, thinking that now he would be received with the honor due a prophet of the Most High God. Instead he was met by a messenger of the queen telling him that she was determined to execute him before 24 hours had passed. From the heights he plunged into the depths, fled for his life, and all alone came to the wilderness of Beer-sheba. As the holy writer tells the story, "He himself went a day's journey into the wilderness and came and sat down under a juniper tree; and he requested for himself that he might die and said, It is enough; now, O Lord, take away my life, for I am not better than my fathers." (1 Kings 19:4)

Better things might have been expected of Elijah, this great man of God, one of two who were taken to heaven without seeing death. Yet here was a man so discouraged, so down-in-the-mouth, that he wanted to die. Life had lost all interest for him because he had yielded completely to his fears. Utterly exhausted, he sat down under that juniper tree and hoped for death: "It is enough; O Lord, take away my life."

You don't have to be an adult to have feelings like that. Young people have them too. It is not uncommon for boys and girls to have those moments of deep depression when they wish they had not been born. Older people too, who have taken every stress and strain in life, can yield to the blues, forgetting those moments when God visited and sustained them.

What made Elijah act the way he did? For one thing, he was physically exhausted. There can be little doubt about this, for right after pouring forth his despair he went to sleep. As he lay and slept under the juniper tree, "an angel touched him and said to him, 'Arise and eat.' And he looked, and behold, there was . . . a cake baked on hot stones, and a jar of water." After eating and drinking, he went to sleep again. Once more the angel "touched him and said: 'Arise and eat, else the journey will be too great for you.' And he arose, and ate and drank, and went in the strength of that food forty days and forty nights to Horeb, the mount of God" (1 Kings 19:5-8). God expects us to take care of ourselves, to provide for the wants of our bodies. That includes sleeping as well as getting the right and proper amounts of food for the sustenance of the body.

Elijah was not out of the woods just because he had been picked up physically. Coming to Mount Horeb, he found a cave and took up his residence there. But he was still in a complaining mood. The word of the Lord came to him: "What are you doing here, Elijah?" Elijah answered, "I have been very jealous for the Lord, the God of hosts, for the people of Israel have forsaken Thy covenant, thrown down Thy altars, and slain Thy prophets with the sword; and I, even I only, am left; and they seek my life to take it away." (1 Kings 19:9-10)

What a lonely man! Little more than forty days before, he had stood before king and people as one who could lick the world. He seemed to be above the necessity of sympathy and companionship—while even our Lord, though He was God, felt the need for the companionship of His friends and was disappointed in the Garden when they let Him down.

Great as he was, Elijah was discouraged because he felt all alone in the battle against irreligion, idolatry, and atheism. In his loneliness he acquired a sort of one-man-against-the-world complex, asserting bluntly that he was the only one left on God's side. Loneliness has a way of bringing people to such a state. This is why it is important to visit people who have recently lost a loved one or have undergone some shattering experience. It is more important in those circumstances to be there and to show friendship than it is to think of something clever to say. Ordinary expressions of kindness have their own keen and curing effect on a heart laid bare by anguish.

Loneliness can be a time of temptation. "I was lonely," is the explanation many a one has given for a breakdown of character that has followed such discouragement. When you are lonely, it is important to remember that God is always at hand. He refuses to be thrust aside even by complaining. When you are lonely, it is important to draw closer to God and to be led by those people who will draw you closer to Him rather than lead you down the devil's way.

Elijah was discouraged because he had been disappointed in his work. He had been sure that the Lord's cause would prevail, yet now he was a fugitive. All his efforts seemed in vain.

Of course he was mistaken. When he repeated his complaint that he was the only one left, God told him to get up and be on his way, to anoint Hazael king over Syria, Jehu king over Israel, and Elisha his own prophetic successor. "Yet I have left Me," said the Lord God, "seven thousand in

Israel, all the knees which have not bowed unto Baal, and every mouth which hath not kissed him." What looks like failure to us may not be failure after all. God has a different way of looking at things. Elijah had helped save a nation from complete surrender to idolatry. In God's view his work had been successful.

Parents sometimes wonder whether sacrifices for their children are worthwhile. Sunday school teachers or youth workers may be discouraged with the results of their work. You may have tried to help a friend with remarkably few evidences of success. You may feel, "I'm a complete failure. I can't see any positive results of what I am doing. I guess I ought to give up." Remember, this is only *your* verdict. You don't know all the facts. God knows them, and His is the final verdict. God does not always tell us what His verdict is, but He expects us to keep on working through discouragement and disappointment, remembering that success is His to define and His to give. He works things out in such a way that our best work and influence often remain unseen by others and even by ourselves, and so keeps us from becoming proud and conceited.

In addition to physical exhaustion, loneliness, and disappointment with his work, there was another reason for Elijah's deep discouragement. He felt that he had let God down. Deep down inside he resented this. He was angry with himself and angry with his God.

Knowledge of our own moral failures, our sins, has a way of bringing on the blues. If you feel that you have not lived up to your own expectations of yourself, not to speak about God's expectations of you, there is a natural tendency to be discouraged, to say to yourself, "What's the use? It doesn't make any difference what I say or do. I'm always wrong, and nobody cares." The devil loves this kind of reaction to personal failure. He will try to bind you hand and foot with the heavy chains of discouragement.

God does not bind; He frees. He tells you He loves you even in your worst moments. In your most disappointing failures you are worth more to Him than silver and gold. You mean so much to Him that He sent His only Son to live just for you and to die just for you on His bloody cross.

Christ did not despair. He stuck with His Father, and His Father stuck with Him. He was obedient unto death. For the joy of this obedience He endured the cross, despising the shame, and was set down at the right hand of God. In your time of despair Christ never says to you, "It's no use. You'll never make it anyway. You can never rise from the mess in which you find yourself." Instead He says: "Though your sins be as scarlet, they shall be white as snow."

In her book *Living Teachers*, Margaret Slattery tells of a young lawyer who came to town to set up his law practice. He impressed people of the town by the melancholy look on his face. When he walked down the street, his head was low, and his face wore a look of distress. One day he confessed to an artist who had a studio in town that in his early years as a lawyer he had committed a terrible wrong that weighed on his conscience.

The artist said little that day. A few weeks later, however, he invited the lawyer to his studio. He had just finished a portrait. When it was unveiled, the lawyer saw it was a portrait of himself — only in this picture he stood straight, his shoulders were thrown back, and his face exuded confidence and hope. The lawyer stared at the portrait for a while and then remarked to himself: "If you see that in me, I ought to be able to see it in myself. If you think I can be that man, then I can be that man. What's more, I shall be that man."

We must see ourselves as God sees us. He looks not at what we are, but at what He can make of us with His grace and power. He does not accept our verdict, our confession of failure, as the last word. He has spoken the last word. He has spoken the last word Himself through His Son, the crucified Savior. Planting trust in Christ the Savior into your heart, God can make of you the kind of person He wants you to be.

Look at God's portrait of yourself. That portrait you will find by looking into the loving face of Christ the Savior. He is everything you should want to be. You cannot become like Christ through your own power, but you can become more like

Him by placing your confidence in Him, accepting His forgiveness, and taking His hand in loving obedience.

Put your trust in Christ, and God will do for you what He did for Elijah. God put Elijah to work, sending him on a mission that made him forget himself and all his discouragements. God cares. He cares about you. An opportunity is waiting for you at this moment to serve Him. It may not be much, perhaps only a smile toward one who is despondent and discouraged. Take it and use it. It is God's way of using you. It is His way of calling to you: "Come out, you, from under that juniper tree."

6

Never Alone

Loneliness is the deep trouble of the human spirit come to the surface. Though a man tries to hide its telltale signs even from his friends and family and tries to banish it from his own consciousness, it is still there gnawing at his heart and pushing its way out into the open at unexpected and often most inopportune moments. To an understanding counselor loneliness helps to explain what people have not been able to explain to themselves: why their faces show pain when they are otherwise well and healthy, why they speak out bitterly when no bitterness can be justified, why they do incomprehensible things and seek undesirable companions although they know the price that must be paid for waywardness and defiance of God's will.

Loneliness makes people dread the isolation of illness and causes them to fear the leisure of old age. It is the agony of the human spirit that can properly be described as hell: an earthly manifestation of hell, the ultimate quality of which is separation from God and the condemnation to live by oneself apart from God.

Of course, loneliness has its good points. It

moves young people to seek each other's company and even to fall in love. It leads men and women to establish homes and communities and even to fall in love with those homes and communities. Still, no matter how good may be some of its effects, none of them can make loneliness appear good. Some of the greatest pain I have seen has been that of boys, away from home for the first time, who could not be comforted in their loneliness despite the presence all around them of friends who wanted to help.

One of the most moving letters I have ever read came from a young man whose facial deformity had caused other people to shun him. In deep loneliness he asked me this pathetic question: "Will I ever find someone to love me?"

Loneliness ought to be recognized for what it is. Whether it is found in a homesick boy, in an aged man whose life's companion has gone on before him, in a working girl looking for companionship in a big city, or in a member of a family that has not learned to share its love, loneliness is the far-off echo of the voice of the Creator whispering to a lost child: "I have made you for Myself, and you will never be complete without Me." The hunger of loneliness can be temporarily satisfied by people and by things, but the deepest urging of an empty life can be filled only by the God who has created that life.

The noise and the clamor of life, the constant and insistent demands made on you by people and by business may have drowned out the voice of God and erased from your consciousness the recognition of His presence. When the demands of life threatened to do that to our Lord, He sought out His Father. He sought Him out alone. On occasion He rose early in the morning and went up into the mountains to be close to Him, to talk to Him and commune with Him.

The last words of the Gospel of St. Matthew, some of the last words ever spoken by our Lord during His earthly sojourn, were directed by our Lord to the loneliness of people: "Lo, I am with you always, even to the end of the world."

God can come closer to us than we can come to each other. It is not exactly unusual for a pastor to discover that people have lived together for forty or fifty years and have never really come to know each other. All of us are prisoners of our own thoughts and feelings, hiding from each other behind the barrier of self, often communicating only on the level of the superficial. As the English poet once said, each of us has those "thoughts too deep for tears."

Have you ever experienced a desperate inner longing to share your deepest self with someone else? Or to have that someone share his or her deepest self with you? Love shares, but the love of which we are capable is always imperfect, and none of us is able to share himself completely. Only One in the history of the world shared Himself completely, because His love was perfect. Why not take Him up on His offer of sharing Himself completely with you: "Lo, I am with you always, even to the end of the world"?

This is God speaking to you: "Deep calls unto deep." "His Spirit talks to our spirit." The language of God begins where words leave off. It goes deeper than the deepest of our thoughts. God speaks to our unspoken yearnings and calms even our unformed fears. His Spirit searches out our secret hearts and responds before we cry. To this reaching out there can be but one response: "Lord, I believe"—unless it be that other response: "Lord, I do not believe."

I remember a man on whose granite features was written the suffering of years. He had been held in solitary confinement solely because of his profession of his faith in Christ. Speaking with deep emotion about this experience, an emotion that was all the more moving because it was deeply controlled within him, he said: "Christ was always with me. I was never alone."

Christ was not exaggerating to make a point or using figurative language when He said: "Lo, I am with you always, even to the end of the world." This is a sacred promise to all who believe in Him —a promise that cannot be broken. Because of Christ's promise, eyes of faith can reach out into the empty blackness and can always see Christ. He is always there. Believers can always say: "I see you, Lord. I know You are there because You promised to be there."

Throw this promise of Christ into the teeth of fear. Loneliness multiplies fear. A few soldiers in a foxhole together will not be nearly as frightened as one all alone. Someone who is afraid to be alone at night can be comforted by the presence of a small child, even by the company of a small puppy. But there are fears we cannot share with others. There are paths we must walk alone — except for God. St. Paul beautifully described the Christian way of life as a walk with Christ. According to Paul, "We are baptized with Christ, we live with Him, we suffer with Him, we are crucified and buried with Him, and we are raised with Him." At every fearful crossroad of life there is a sign that says: "Jesus Christ went this way." Seeing that sign and hearing His promise, "Lo, I am with you always," we know that He goes with us today.

The lonesomeness of life cannot be solved simply by joining a club or organization, by throwing yourself into community activities, or by allowing yourself to become completely absorbed in business. There will always be those dark corners that refuse to be illuminated, that become darker as time goes on.

God answers your loneliness by making you a member of His family. He makes you His son or daughter through faith in His Son, Jesus Christ. To have faith in Christ is to believe in Him, to trust Him completely, to put your confidence in Him, to take Him at His word. He said: "I am come to seek and to save that which was lost." He said: "Whoever believes in Me shall not perish but have everlasting life." He said: "Lo, I am with you always." Believe in Christ, and come to know the light and warmth of home.

It does not matter how far you have wandered away from God or how long you have been away. God has been looking for you all the while. That is why Jesus Christ came into the world. He lived for you. He died for you. He was raised from the dead to be your Lord. Put yourself into His hands. He puts Himself into your hands: "Lo, I am with you always, even to the end of the world." He says, "Follow Me; I shall lead you through. I know the way; I have traveled it for you."

Christ's presence in your life means more than a shared experience. His presence is a guarantee of the power to fight the battle of life. In a well-known fantasy one of the characters is quoted as saying: "I always do six impossible things before breakfast." It may seem to you that God expects you to do a hundred impossible things every day. He asks you to love in a world seething with hate. He asks you to live in an unseen world where the eternal things count, while the urgencies of the visible world try to absorb your energies completely. He asks you to witness for Him among people who are indifferent to Him. He asks you to hope when the situation looks hopeless; to have faith when everything calls you to disbelieve. He asks you to sacrifice in a society based on getting things. He asks you to deny yourself, to follow the plain way of the cross. He asks you to do this on the strength of His own great promise: "Lo, I am with you always."

This promise was made to eleven ordinary men, most of them fishermen and common laborers, to whom He had just given an impossible assignment: "Go and make disciples of the whole world." Before they could protest, He was gone. He ascended into heaven and to all intents and purposes left them alone. I can just imagine how they felt as they went down that mountain. "First He tells us to convert the world, and then He leaves us." Ten days later they found out what He meant. He had said: "Lo, I am with you always, even to the end of the world." Ten days later the power of the Spirit of God descended upon them, and cowardice was replaced with courage, doubt with burning enthusiasm. Stammering tongues became eloquent, and feeble hearts were filled with heroic faith. This is the power of the presence that He offers: "Lo, I am with you always."

I know this seems like nonsense to people who have become accustomed to regard life as purely ordinary. But I am referring to the extraordinary quality that comes into life with faith in Jesus Christ, the extraordinary quality that comes from His living presence, as He promised: "Lo, I am with you always, even to the end of the world."

When Christ says to you, "Repent; change your life; follow Me," He is standing right there offering you the power to do the impossible — the power that changed the dying thief, made a spokesman for God out of an impulsive coward, transformed a persecutor into an apostle, and turned thousands of hopeless people into confident believers. It is the power of His unseen presence.

You may be tempted to say, "I can't change; I can't believe; I can't hope." He invites you to throw away those doubts and hesitations. Believe in Him. He is standing at your elbow, drawing you to Himself. Look up at Him. His outstretched arms, raised in blessing upon you, cast the shadow of His cross on your life. Look up at Him and live.

7

No Reason to Worry

In the classic story of the mad knight Don Quixote, the hero's companion, Sancho Panza, clings all night in fear to the ledge of a window — only to discover at daybreak that his feet are but an inch from the ground.

Some of the people who laugh at this incident might just as well be laughing at themselves. "Ledge gripping," or, to use a more familiar term, worrying, is a highly developed and often soul-destroying aptitude. All kinds of people, in every walk of life, are petrified with fear, clinging to ledges of doubt, grasping skeptical half-truths of certainty, succeeding only in prolonging the days of their agony.

God did not intend that people, whom He created and redeemed, should hang suspended that way between life and death, dependent on their own ability and their own endurance to overcome the perils in which they find themselves or in which they think they find themselves.

God's answer to the problems of living, including the problems of making a living, is emphatically stated in the words of Christ: "Seek ye first the kingdom of God and His righteousness, and all these things shall be added unto you." (Matt. 6:33)

This is good news. Christ was talking about living. He was talking to people who were anxious about the ordinary problems of making a living, preoccupied with anxieties about food, clothing, and shelter. He might have said, as some of the practitioners of peace of mind do today, "Don't worry! There's nothing to worry about." That would be just about as ineffective as telling a person: "Don't catch a cold." Christ understood people and their deepest needs better than that. He understood that the deepest need of man is his need for God. He understood, too, that God's presence, God's help, and God's forgiveness are essential if a man is to enjoy a life free from the nagging concerns of a troubled conscience and the cares of living.

Worry is not, as some people seem to think, an essential ingredient for the maintenance of life. It has no nutritional value for the body or for the soul. On the contrary, worry plays havoc with life. A large industrial concern discovered that nine out of ten cases of workers' inefficiency were caused by worry. A life insurance company found that four out of five nervous breakdowns began not in actual events but in worry about what might happen. A medical clinic's analysis of its patients showed that 35% of all illnesses on its records started with worry. Just as a cold is a symptom of a deficiency that exists in the body, so is worry the symptom of a crippling disease that invades the soul. That disease is lack of faith in God.

There is a God. There is only one God. He is the God who rules the world. Not a thing exists in the world that was not made by Him. Every single discovery of man, every article that has ever been manufactured, utilizes material that came directly from the hand of God.

That people should want to take the place of God, to rule in His stead, to take everything He has given them into their own hands, and to organize their lives to suit themselves without regard for others and most of all without regard for God, seems to be the height of insanity. Yet it is exactly what an enormous lot of people are doing. It may be what you are doing.

If you are living your life that way, without God or in defiance of Him, you have good reason for worry. You do not know where to turn when you get into trouble. Slanderous gossip, annoyances in business, family troubles, or anxiety about your finances get you down. People worry about everything except God.

But if people have not been worrying about God, He has been worrying about them. Indeed, He turned the tables on mankind and took our place in the person of His Son, Jesus Christ. He took all our guilt, all our guilty feelings, all our worries on Himself. God has always been King; but He established His kingdom, His rule, among men in a special way through the life, death, and resurrection of His Son, Jesus Christ. In love He invites us to believe in the validity of Christ's sacrifice for our sins, in His gracious offer to save us from ourselves and from all our troubles, in His generous willingness to relieve us of our cares and our worries. This includes, our Lord wants us to know, even the necessities of life. He is the Lord of *all* of life.

Knowing His Father, Christ found it hard to understand that people would spend their time worrying. "Put first things first," He said. "Seek first the kingdom of God and His righteousness, and all of these things (that is, all of the ordinary necessities of life) will be added unto you."

Put first things first, said Christ. Remember God, trust in Him, depend on Him, and He will take care of you. In His characteristically homely way Christ told us to look at the birds of the air. They neither sow nor reap, yet God does not let them starve. If God feeds the birds, don't you think He will provide for you, to whom He has given the ability to sow and to reap, to reason and to work?

Think of the lilies, the flowers of the field. Put the finest fabric ever loomed through a microscopic examination, and it will look like burlap sack alongside the drapery with which God clothes the lilies of the field. There is not a petal which in exquisite finish and perfection would not put to shame all the robes ever worn by the best-dressed man and the best-dressed woman. Surely, said Christ, He who clothes the lilies of the field will clothe His children too. Put first things first, and all of these things will cause you no worry at all.

Some people insist there is only one proper way to learn to swim. You begin, so to speak, "by faith." You start with the dead man's float. You wade out waist-deep, take a deep breath, stretch your arms and hands straight out before you, and lie face down in the water. Your feet come up straight out behind. You cannot sink. You float. You are not holding yourself up. You make no effort of your own. If you struggle, in fact, you sink. The water says in effect, "If you will let me, I will bear you up." You relax and faith does it. By faith you come out on top.

This is a parable. God extends an offer: "I will float you." You answer, "Float me," and He does. You have only to know God to depend on Him. As E. Stanley Jones once put it, "Let go, and let God."

Worry has a way of sapping a man's strength so that he can't think and he can't work. God has given each of us an intellect to use in planning our work and solving our problems. He has given us energy to carry out our tasks, and initiative to employ the opportunities He Himself places before us. He wants us to do our thinking and our working without worrying. That's why He has promised to sustain us.

To prevent worry from spoiling your life, Christ advises you, "Seek God's kingdom and His righteousness first." You will note that Christ does not say, "Seek only God's kingdom and His righteousness." Rather does He say, "Seek God's kingdom and righteousness first."

In His own prayer, Christ taught us to pray: "Thy kingdom come." In the Lord's Prayer Christ focused our attention first on God's name, God's kingdom, God's will. I've heard people say, "I never prayed so hard in my life." What was it that made them pray that way? Was someone in the family seriously sick? Was some disaster impending? What are the things for which you have prayed fervently? A better job, a better home, a richer life, friendship, protection? I would not criticize you for praying for any one of these things, but are they the first things for which Christ has urged us to pray?

Christ Himself explained that petition, "Thy kingdom come," with the next one: "Thy will be done on earth as it is in heaven." Are you praying that God's will be done in you? Do you pray that His will be done in the world? Are you praying for Christian missionaries at home and abroad, those hearty men and women who are so badly needed and who so earnestly desire your prayers? Are you praying that the Good News which has entered your heart will enter the hearts of others also? Are you praying that God will make you a missionary, a witness for Christ?

None of us is perfect. Even seeking God and His righteousness, we shall find that we make mistakes, that we fail to achieve our highest hopes. That's why Christ directs us to God's righteousness. God's righteousness comes to us through Christ. Christ assumed our sins. He made Himself responsible for our failures. When Christ died, our sin, our imperfection, was placed on Him. In turn His perfect righteousness was transferred to us. This must be the greatest transaction that has ever taken place in human history. Believe that, and stake your life on it.

When Christ says, "Seek first God's kingdom and His righteousness," He means: Seek God to rule your life, and seek to be regarded as righteous by God through trusting in Christ your Savior. These are the things we ought to seek first of all and to pray for first of all. After Christ taught us to pray, "Thy kingdom come, Thy will be done," He added: "Give us this day our daily bread." Bread, clothing, shelter — all these things will be added to you if you put first things first. Christ promises it: God will see to it that you get the other things you need, and you don't have to worry about them.

A little boy was once asked, "What is salt?" He replied promptly, "Salt is what spoils the potatoes when you leave it out." So it is with Christian faith. Christian faith is what spoils everything — when you leave it out. The tears and fears of life, the tragedies and care of living, from which so many people suffer, are but the rash that breaks out on the surface of life when the bloodstream of our purpose is poisoned or weak or anemic. If things are wrong at the center of life, then things will be wrong too at the circumference of life. Make Christ the center of your life, and everything else will be all right too. Christ says so, and He does not lie. Free yourself from the fretting, the friction, and the feverishness of life. Go to God before you go to pieces. Don't get sidetracked on the detours of life. Get on the straight road, the road of God's good and gracious purpose for you, the road of faith in God.

Work hard to earn a living, but depend on God to see you through. Trust in God. You have no reason to worry about anything.

8

A Case of Nerves

"It's just a case of nerves."

How often you hear that these days — "Just a case of nerves." This short phrase describes one of the most common complaints of our time, ranging all the way from simple tension to complete mental collapse. No wonder the tranquilizer business is booming.

There has probably never been a time in history when so many people have been afflicted with a case of nerves. As one national news magazine said, "Anxiety seems to be the dominant note of modern life."

Nerves are not new, of course. Every age has presented people with its own set of anxieties, and there have always been people constitutionally unable to meet the severe tests they were subjected to.

The modern age, however, has seen the development of what may be described as mass psychosis. People live in constant fear of things at home and things abroad, of what may happen and of what could happen again, of what others can do or of what they themselves may do to wreck their own little world.

We know a great deal more today than most of our ancestors could possibly have known about the physical and mental makeup of man. I have not noticed, however, that all the discoveries about the circulation of blood and about the various properties of blood have ended the danger of heart attacks. Indeed, there may be more heart attacks today than ever before in history.

We know more about the inner workings of man's mind than did our great-grandfathers or anybody who preceded them. Yet we are less prepared to bear up under the shocks of life and to take them bravely than were many of our grandparents.

We talk more about nerves today than any people in the history of the world. Perhaps we have more to talk about. Soaring divorce rates, runaway crime figures, and the increasing number of alcoholics, illegitimate births, and suicides all point to a world wandering aimlessly about, having lost its bearings.

People crowd into cities, and the pace of life quickens. Life in the large cities of the world, which are constantly becoming larger, has an unnerving effect on people. As the pace accelerates, people are thrown together in a hurly-burly that becomes less personal, increasingly more like a machine, and consequently more unsettling for men and women everywhere who were raised to expect something quite different.

Think for a moment of the ambitious, young

executive who is caught up in the competitive struggle of modern organizational man; or of his wife, trying to fulfill her destiny as a woman, finding housekeeping neither creative nor time-consuming, and relieving her boredom through contrived activities of the social club; or of their children, who are pushed to do better and better work at school and to be more adept at sports or social dating than is suitable for boys and girls of their tender years. While we are at it, let's toss in the college graduate who moves to the city to begin a career and finds escape from loneliness in circles where religion and morality are considered a joke; or the family on welfare row because automation has ousted the father from his job and he can't find another one because he's no longer young and wasn't trained in any special skills; or the elderly couple waiting out their years in a lonely two-room apartment, afraid of life and afraid of death. Add to these the teen-age dropout from school, the respectable husband who is cheating on his wife, the successful man or woman looking for some worthwhile thing to do in life and finding none, and you get a rough sketch of some of the pressures that bring about a first-class case of nerves.

The pressures of life are strong. Usually they are in the wrong direction. Sometimes they are impersonal pressures, and at other times they are extremely personal, creating a deep sense of guilt over having violated a sacred trust or, just as deadly, developing a deep depression with the growing realization that one is growing older and time is growing shorter.

With all the pressures people have to withstand in the modern world, something has gone out of modern life, giving our world the jitters, a first-class case of nerves such as history has seldom seen. A well-known psychiatrist has summarized the situation in this way: "What is it that has happened to the neatly ordered world of fifty years ago that causes so much anxiety for today's graduate?" The French atheist philosopher Jean Paul Sartre analyzes the dilemma well. The scientists at the turn of the century thought God a useless and costly hypothesis, Sartre says, but they decided it would be necessary to maintain the Christian moral code to keep civilization functioning in an orderly manner. They believed it really didn't make any difference if God didn't exist; things would run on just the same. But things haven't, and there's the rub!

If the almighty God of the Bible does not exist to define in absolute terms the purpose and meaning of life, there is no one to tell us. We cannot appeal to others, for each person is as fallible as the next. We cannot appeal to ourselves, for even our simplest daily decisions are fraught with bias, prejudice, and unwitting self-deception. The Bible says, "The heart of man is desperately wicked and deceitful above all things; who can know it?"

For many people, God has vanished, and there

is no one to take His place. People cannot distinguish right from wrong, because God is not there to provide the standards. People do not even know what makes them men, because they have denied the God who made them. Not knowing what to do or what not to do, they fall quite naturally into a restless sea of anxiety, uncertainty, and fear.

The apostle Paul was not a psychiatrist, but he had an answer — a good answer — the only real answer — to the anxieties and fears of people in every age. "Have no anxiety," said Paul. "Is that what he said?" Yes, that's what he said: "Have no anxiety."

What kind of advice is that? Is it some more of this peace-of-mind business, which people are supposed to acquire by thinking positive and happy thoughts? No, St. Paul was not a philosopher trying to get inside man's mind, telling him what he ought to think. What is more, this man had too great a respect for the problems people are constantly battling to serve up to them some ineffectual and pious sentimentality.

There is nothing sentimental about Paul's advice: "The Lord is near; have no anxiety, but in everything make your requests known to God in prayer and petition with thanksgiving. Then the peace of God, which is beyond our utmost understanding, will keep guard over your hearts and your thoughts, in Christ Jesus." (Phil. 4:6-7 NEB)

God cares. Never forget it! God cares about you. You can depend on it! No matter what, God will care for you. You can rely on Him!

Turn over your cares and your anxieties to God, and be thankful to Him that He exists. "The Lord is near; have no anxiety, but in everything make your requests known to God in prayer and petition with thanksgiving."

Isn't all this talk about God incredibly naive in the face of the terrifying complexities and uncertainties of modern life? Not at all. The man who wrote this advice was having a complex life himself. He probably wrote these words from a prison cell, not from an easy chair in front of a comfortable fireplace. He is handing out strong meat instead of the predigested oatmeal people want to be fed these days.

Don't be taken in by your anxieties, says Paul, because God is near, nearer than you think. Your Creator is your Redeemer. He wants you for His own, in the circle of His own family, relying on Him and striding through the troubled waters of life with courage and hope. "Cast all your cares upon Him," said the apostle Peter, "for He cares for you." So He does! St. Paul took God at His word. A cold stone floor and iron bars cannot imprison the heart that depends on God.

In his younger years Paul had kicked hard against God, and God came to meet him—came to meet him directly—in the person of His Son, Jesus Christ. This is the way God meets people all the time—in Jesus Christ.

The unyielding young man submitted himself to Christ in faith. He really believed. Christ the crucified Savior, Christ the risen Lord, stayed with Paul through thick and thin. What had been repugnant to Saul became quite the thing to do for Paul. He followed Christ, having found in Christ forgiveness of sins and a new purpose in life. What else can a man have, when all is said and done, than the sure knowledge that his sins are forgiven and that life has a purpose?

In this same letter to the Philippians, Paul described what happened to him after he came to know Christ as his Savior: "Every advantage that I had gained I considered loss for Christ's sake. Yes, and I look upon everything as loss compared with the overwhelming gain of knowing Christ Jesus my Lord. For His sake I did in actual fact suffer the loss of everything, but I considered it useless rubbish compared with being able to win Christ. For now my place is in Him, and I am not dependent upon any of the self-achieved righteousness of the Law. God has given me that genuine righteousness which comes from faith in Christ. How changed are my ambitions! Now I long to know Christ and the power shown by His resurrection; now I long to share His sufferings, even to die as He died, so that I may perhaps attain, as He did, the resurrection from the dead." (Phil. 3:7-11 Phillips)

Christ died for you; Christ rose from the dead for you. This is true. Don't go on living as if it were not true. "The Lord is near; have no anxiety, but in everything make your requests known to

God in prayer and petition with thanksgiving. Then the peace of God, which is beyond our utmost understanding, will keep guard over your hearts and your thoughts, in Christ Jesus."

Christ lives. Pray therefore with all confidence to be relieved of every burden that lies on your heart, constantly giving thanks to God for just the fact that He is a God to whom you can pray. Pray without pride, for pride is an evidence of fear and weakness. There is no room for pride in any prayer that petitions God to let His power be known in your life.

Cast your care and anxiety upon God. The peace of God, which is beyond our utmost understanding, will stand guard over your heart and mind in Christ Jesus.

With mind and heart fixed upon God in Christ Jesus, enjoy a peace that is past all understanding, the peace of God Himself. You don't have to understand it, but you can know it. Know the peace of God that comes from letting God do the worrying.

Many people want to know God, but they won't take Him except on their own terms. They are perfectly willing to try God, but they want to understand first of all how He operates. They are willing to accept the truth that probably God gives peace, but they have to know how the peace works. They want to call the shots themselves, and then they will go along.

You can't turn the tables on God. This is God's

way: First put yourself in His hands through prayer and petition with thanksgiving, accepting His grace because He gives it and His goodness because He shows it, and then you will have peace. God is not a cosmic healer dispensing spiritual tranquilizers. He is a God who offers peace — peace beyond our utmost understanding.

For this Christ came, that you might have peace. Born in a stable, executed on a cross, He did all for you. Risen from the dead and declared to be the Son of God with power, He is near. Have no anxiety. To you He gives His good word: "Peace I leave with you; My peace I give unto you; not as the world gives do I give unto you." He means it! Take Him at His word.

No anesthetic, this! No aspirin and no tranquilizer! No cheap imitation peace does He bring. Moved with compassion for people just like you, He touches jittery nerves with His healing power. Accept Christ for what He really is, your Lord and Savior. Know that He is near.

"The Lord is near; have no anxiety, but in everything make your requests known to God in prayer and petition with thanksgiving. Then the peace of God, which is beyond our utmost understanding, will keep guard over your hearts and your thoughts, in Christ Jesus."

9

A Wholesome Fear

It is no disgrace to admit that at some time or other you have been afraid. Anyone who claims never to have known fear is either a fool or a liar.

Fear can be a healthy and beneficial emotion. It can alert the senses to danger, and it can stimulate into action. It must have been with some such feeling about fear that a renowned atomic scientist said to the whole world four months after the first atomic bomb was dropped, "We need first of all to be thoroughly frightened."

It isn't bad for children to be afraid of fire.

It is wise to look out for the undertow when swimming.

You may have heard someone say that he fears "neither God nor man." You can be sure that a person who talks that way is just trying to build up a feeling of self-importance.

Jesus Christ was not trying to build up anyone's sense of his own importance but simply recognizing one of the facts of life when He said, "Fear not them which kill the body but are not able to kill the soul; but rather fear Him which is able to destroy both soul and body in hell" (Matt. 10:28).

The writer of the Epistle to the Hebrews looked at God realistically and came up with this laconic statement: "It is a fearful thing to fall into the hands of the living God." (Heb. 10:21)

Other people have heard God described as a God of love. Plaintively they inquire why anyone should fear God if He is a God of love. To hear them talk, you would think they have discovered a new truth: that fear of God must be discarded from true worship with the revelation that God is a God of love.

People who talk about God in that way have never inquired into the price of love. In almost every instance you will find they have little understanding of Christ's atonement and crucifixion, of the price He paid for the sins of mankind.

In fact, you will find that people who want to rule out fear of God have little understanding of sin. If they condescendingly allow you and me to retain the word "sin" in our vocabularies, they will disparage a personal sense of sin as one of our quirks, and they will refuse to acknowledge a personal sense of sin themselves.

To minimize sin is to minimize the sacrifice of Christ for sin. To minimize His sacrificial suffering and death for the sins of mankind is to minimize the wrath of God against sin which made Christ's sacrifice necessary. Minimizing the wrath of God against sin, whether yours or mine, whether the sin of a Christian or of a non-Christian, makes it possible for someone to say that God is Love and

He need not be regarded with that holy fear and reverence which both the Old and the New Testaments hold forth as an essential part of true worship of God.

Who can forget the parting injunctions of Moses to Israel?

"And now, Israel, what doth the Lord thy God require of thee but to fear the Lord thy God, to walk in all His ways, and to love Him and to serve the Lord thy God with all thy heart and with all thy soul?" (Deut. 10:12)

The prophets repeated the wholesomeness of fear of God:

"Sanctify the Lord of hosts Himself; and let Him be your fear, and let Him be your dread." (Is. 8:13)

Let no one say that fear of God is a concept of the Old Testament but is not to be found in the New Covenant. Peter wrote explicitly in his First Epistle: "Honor all men. Love the brotherhood. Fear God." (1 Peter 2:17)

Martin Luther reflected the whole attitude of the Scriptures toward God in his explanation of the First Commandment: "Thou shalt have no other gods before Me." This, he said, is what the First Commandment means: "We should fear, love, and trust in God above all things."

Obviously, in our relations with God there is room—indeed, there is the necessity—for a wholesome fear that is not incompatible with love and trust. It is possible for a man to fear God and to love and trust Him at the same time.

When a man deals with God, he had better make up his mind that God is not going to change. He is going to remain God. He is the God who shook Mount Sinai with His power and warned His chosen people not to touch the mountain, for He had taken possession of it.

It will always be true of Him, as St. Paul said: "The wrath of God is revealed from heaven against all ungodliness and unrighteousness of men." (Rom. 1:18)

It will always be true, too, that He is a God of love — approachable, ready to hear, as the psalmist sang of Him: "The eyes of the Lord are upon the righteous, and His ears are open unto their cry." (Ps. 34:15)

God is just as approachable as Jesus Christ made Him out to be, as Jesus Christ Himself showed Him to be. Jesus Christ was sent into the world to be the price of love, to bring the sacrifice necessary to save the world, to be the Mediator between God and man, to be the sinner's Friend. He was the embodiment of God's love and mercy, willing to take the suffering and penalty of a whole world's sin upon Himself to become our Savior. Let no one dare to take God's justice and power lightly after what happened to Jesus Christ. And let no one take His mercy and love for granted after seeing what happened to Jesus Christ. That is what the Epistle to the Hebrews points out, chapter 12, verses 25 to 29:

"See that you do not refuse Him who is speaking. For if they did not escape when they refused Him who warned them on earth, much less shall we escape if we reject Him who warns from heaven. His voice then shook the earth; but now He has promised, 'Yet once more I will shake not only the earth but also the heaven.' This phrase, 'Yet once more,' indicates the removal of what is shaken, as of what has been made, in order that what cannot be shaken may remain. Therefore let us be grateful for receiving a kingdom that cannot be shaken, and thus let us offer to God acceptable worship, with reverence and awe; for our God is a consuming fire."

The logic of this Word of God is inescapable. Created things, even though God created them, will not last. Only what is eternal will go on world without end.

What kind of values do you have? What you would hate to lose will determine what you fear. If you set a great value on the things that can be "shaken," as the text puts it, the things that never last, you are going to react to life a good deal differently from the person who realizes that material possessions, and even our present world, belong to things that he can take or leave, because he has set his heart on the things that cannot be shaken, the things that will remain.

What's the good of worrying about gadgets when all they do is to make the merry-go-round of life go a little faster? Why should you allow yourself to become so terribly concerned about clothing and food and shelter?

All these things that people look on as so important will pass away, but God remains. One day God will shake the earth and the heavens as He once shook Mount Sinai. "Yet once more," He says, and the things that can be shaken will be shaken off, and only what cannot be shaken will remain.

What is it that cannot be shaken? The writer to the Hebrews says, "Let us be grateful for receiving a kingdom that cannot be shaken."

A kingdom of which you can be proud to be a citizen, and for which you can be grateful, was established by Jesus Christ. God sent Christ into this transient world to carve out a commonwealth, a "city of the living God," an "assembly of the firstborn who are enrolled in heaven." When you come to God, you come to the "Judge who is God of all," and you come to "Jesus, the Mediator of a new covenant, and to the sprinkled blood of Christ that speaks more graciously than the blood of Abel," who, like Christ, died innocently at the hand of his brother.

The commonwealth of God is a blood-bought kingdom that has its origin and derives its power from the cross of Christ. To belong, to claim citizenship in the realm that cannot be shaken, you need to be redeemed. And you have been re-deemed—that is what God is saying to you. He says so in the person of Jesus Christ, who died that you might live. "See that you do not refuse Him who is speaking. For if they did not escape when they refused Him who warned them on earth, much less shall we escape if we reject Him who warns from heaven. His voice then shook the earth; but now He has promised, 'Yet once more I will shake not only the earth but also the heaven.' This phrase, 'Yet once more,' indicates the removal of what is shaken, as of what has been made, in order that what cannot be shaken may remain. Therefore let us be grateful for receiving a kingdom that cannot be shaken, and thus let us offer to God acceptable worship, with reverence and awe; for our God is a consuming fire."

Whom do you fear? That's a question you will have to answer.

Do you want so desperately to be accepted by your friends and associates that out of fear—let's face it, that's what it is—out of fear you will go along with their standards, their opinions, their values, even though it means forgetting God and abandoning your one hope for a life free from nameless and unexplainable fears? Or are you going to listen to God—listen to Him with awe and reverence and fear—a fear that you can understand because He is God?

Our God is a consuming fire. He will one day cauterize away all evil, all selfishness, all sin. He is a God of justice and truth, ready to shake what today appears unshakable.

Our God is a consuming fire. In the fire of Christ's death and atonement He has saved the world. When He raised Jesus Christ from the dead,

He established a kingdom of the saved — a kingdom that cannot be shaken. Do you want a new life? Come to Christ and be saved — safe from the consequences of your sin — safe eternally. Do you want to be freed from fear? Come to Christ and become God's friend. Say to God, "I accept Your gift of a Savior. I take Christ for my own, and I want to be Your obedient son, I want to be Your loving child." Say that with awe and reverence and fear right now, and you will be offering to God acceptable worship, the kind He loves to receive, the kind on which He loves to bestow blessing.

10

Nothing to Live For

Judas committed suicide, one of five people in the Bible — all men — who took their own lives, with the possible addition of two others destroyed by their own hands. That makes seven in all, over several thousand years covered by Bible narrative.

Each year, in the United States alone, over 23,000 people take their own lives, not to speak about those who do the same in other countries throughout the world. Suicides occur in the United States at the rate of about 60 a day, and one can only guess what the worldwide figures must be. These are people who openly and avowedly took their own lives; the figure does not include what authorities call "hidden suicides," which have been estimated by reputable authorities to be five times as numerous as the official figures would indicate. Obviously suicide and the causes that bring it about constitute a world problem of enormous proportions comparable only to the casualty figures of the two great world wars fought in our century.

The urge to self-destruction is no respecter of persons. It is not restricted to people of any one economic status, of any particular race or national origin. Old people and young people, educated and uneducated, rich and poor are to be found among those listed in the newspapers as possible or probable suicides — people like ourselves, who have decided that the only way out is to end it all.

Whatever it is that drives people to suicide, it is not superficial. Whatever the cause or causes, they are deep within the minds of people, hidden from the world, in many cases hidden even from the people who take their own lives. There is one common denominator, however: people who commit suicide may have everything to live *with* but nothing to live *for*.

In this they have a lot of company. Millions of people throughout the world are living constantly in a state of deep dejection. Every decision they make comes from a soul that is cast down, and every thought they have is born in a mind that is disquieted within them. Having nothing to live for, they have nothing to die for either. So they live, as we say, from hand to mouth, amid a bleak devastation of spirit which only by the wildest stretch of the imagination can be called "life."

There are many plausible reasons for the deep dejection that has taken the heart out of life in the 20th century. At the end of World War I, after a tremendous struggle that cost the lives of millions of men whose broken bodies lay in the cold and stubborn mud of trenches on the western

90

front, people thought that finally peace had been won. As it turned out, they were badly mistaken. Following the titanic struggle of World War II, which saw additional millions of lives sacrificed to the god of war, people had some expectation that now finally the hope of peace would be realized. Again they were mistaken.

The aftermath of two great world wars, of the bitter cold war, and several more local wars has been the rise of communism and other fanaticisms whose unreasoned approaches to every problem make people feel there is no hope.

With the increase of population all over the world, a new form of mass civilization has developed which hovers on the edge of mass barbarism, where the individual easily comes to feel that he counts for little or nothing. The result has been a thoroughgoing pessimism, which sees the greed and selfishness, the pride and envy, the brutality and hate at large in the world and throws up its hands, saying, "The world is doomed."

Pessimism has had its say for a long time, but now there are atomic bombs, jet planes, and rocket-driven spaceships to back up all the dire predictions of the prophets of doom. The only advice one well-known philosopher has been able to give to our contemporaries is this: "Build as firmly as possible on the foundations of unyielding despair." All of this has given a new twist to the ancient question of St. Paul: "Who shall deliver me from this body of death?"

Out of despair, Judas committed suicide. Love of money probably brought him to this point, but it was not money that caused his despair. His world had collapsed around him. He went out into the night, which became to him the eternal black night of self-destruction.

The problem of Judas was guilt. This is the problem of our world today. All men experience guilt, whether they recognize it for what it is or not.

Guilt is what a man finds when he looks inside himself. The trouble with many people today is that they refuse to look inside themselves. The journey into self is always painful. There are painful memories most of us would like to forget. There are painful realities people desperately try to cover up. When a man looks inside himself and sees nothing at all, he is in serious trouble. Plagued with guilt, he does not even know what is the matter with him. He just knows he has nothing to live for, the end product of desperate despair.

When Judas looked inside himself, he encountered a dark abyss, without hope, without love, without forgiveness. The night into which Judas walked was not nearly as dark as the night inside himself. When people say their life is empty, what they really mean is that they themselves are empty.

Without knowing exactly what is wrong, people all over the world know that something is wrong — something is wrong with themselves. As so often happens, self-condemnation leads to self-distrust, which turns into self-despair, and finally to self-loathing. This is the hell in which millions of people are living today. Pride ends in dejection, and the end of dejection is death. If the wages of sin is death, this is wages collected with interest.

When it comes right down to it, guilt is at the bottom of the whole business. All kinds of things make people feel guilty. It is not necessary to enumerate them here. Abject loneliness is the result, but it is not the problem. The problem is guilt — made worse when it is not recognized for what it really is and for what it does to a man.

When James Forrestal, former Secretary of Defense of the United States, jumped out of a hospital window, he left by his bedside a book of Greek poetry opened to one of the choruses in Sophocles' play *Ajax:*

When Reason's day
Sets rayless — joyless — quenched in cold decay,
Better to die and sleep
The never-waking sleep than linger on
And dare to live when the soul's life is gone.

This is the pessimism of a world with nothing to live for. It is often the natural consequence of guilt unrecognized or, if recognized, without any possibility of being remitted. This is the pessimism of a world that does not consider forgiveness to be possible.

Just because feelings of guilt are so common

today and cause so much difficulty, it is popular to consider them bad. From professional psychiatrists to the man on the street comes the advice, "Get rid of these feelings of guilt." It is just that simple, so people think. Get rid of your feelings of guilt, and your problems will be solved.

Looked at realistically, guilt feelings are not necessarily bad. They are always painful, of course. But pain has a purpose. The feeling of pain can keep you from burning off your hand when you put it into the fire, and a feeling of guilt can keep you from destroying your life without even knowing what you are doing.

The problem of leprosy, or Hansen's disease, is that it destroys feeling in certain extremities of the body and prevents a person from feeling pain. A man so afflicted, for example, can turn a tight lid off a jar which would balk the efforts of any healthy man with the capacity of feeling pain. However, he can wreck his hand in the process. Many a life has been wrecked because no guilt was felt at the moment, though it came on with a rush later on. Many another life has been wrecked by deep feelings of guilt, unrelieved and unremitted because there appeared to be no solution to the problem it presented — no answer to its accusations, no forgiveness to give hope of something better.

Judas went out into the night and threw his blood money at the feet of the authorities with whom he had conspired. "I have sinned against innocent blood," he cried out desperately. They told him, "That is not our business. It is your business." There was no one to hear this man's cry for help.

A cry for help is characteristic of people contemplating suicide. Before taking the fatal step, almost everyone turns in desperation to someone else in search for help. It may be a phone call, a half-disguised word or gesture, a suggestion that can easily be taken as simply a form of bravado, but there is usually something that gives a hint of the desperation that can take hold of a man's mind and soul.

Judas went to the wrong people for help. Though he had been with the Lord, he did not really know Him. Pride or guilt or greed blinded him to what was obvious. Christ can help. In Him there is always help. There is hope and help in the crucified Christ who Himself cried out in the moment of desperation, "My God, My God, why hast Thou forsaken Me?" If Judas heard that cry, for him it was the end. To millions of others who have heard that cry, it has been the beginning of new faith, new life, new hope, and new love.

The cross of Christ has a purpose. St. Paul expressed it in words that have come with healing power in moments of great desperation: "There is therefore now no condemnation for those who are in Christ Jesus." No condemnation—this is what St. Paul said. This is the Good News. It is meant for all. It is meant for you, whoever you are. "There is now no condemnation for those who are in Christ Jesus." (Rom. 8:1)

No dream, this! The cross of Christ is not a dream. It really happened. He really died, as only a man can die—a real man, altogether innocent of any crime, any sin, any guilt. That's the way He died—the one extraordinary death in all of human history.

Men have died before, innocent of the crimes with which they were charged. No man ever died before, and none has died since, entirely free from the accusation of any kind of guilt. That's the way Christ died. He died for us. "There is now no condemnation for those who are in Christ Jesus."

A work on the problem of suicide, called *The Cry for Help*, states that most suicides occur among men in the 40 to 55 age range. This is the period when many men have totally exhausted their physical and emotional capital and are psychologically bankrupt. Bright hopes and dreams of youth gone, defenses and pretenses begin to crumble. All that is left is a terrible, hollow emptiness.

This same emptiness, even though it does not result in suicide, characterizes the lives of millions of people throughout the world. This is what happens when men declare themselves independent of God. Life becomes an empty, haunted house.

The result is what we see all about us, where nothing is settled and nothing can really be said about it.

According to Paul Tournier, a Swiss psychiatrist, almost all adults who come into psychotherapy today are seeking a substitute for the God whom modern man has tried to outgrow. People are urged today not to talk about God anymore. As a result they seek to satisfy their deepest yearnings in camouflage — camouflaged love, camouflaged knowledge, camouflaged confession and absolution.

Forgiveness cannot be camouflaged. Either you accept it or you reject it. The forgiveness of God doesn't have to be camouflaged. It is there for all to see in the cross of Christ, where He was brutally executed for the sins of the world. It is there for all to take in the offer of Christ's Gospel: "There is now no condemnation for those who are in Christ Jesus." It is there to give life with new surging power that comes from faith in Christ to fill the emptiness of the old house haunted with guilt.

No man is too desperate to be saved by the power of Christ. No life is too empty to be revived by the power of the living Christ. I could give you one example after the other of desperate and hopeless people who found new meaning and new hope through faith in Christ. Driven into the ground by their desperate feelings of guilt, often unrecognized, they have been raised to their feet, broken and bleeding, by faith in the One who bled and was broken for them.

Someone has said that the first word of God begins after the last human word has been spoken. The last word of human weakness is the first word of divine strength. The last word of human desperation is the first word of divine hope. With faith in Christ, man's last day becomes God's first day.

Don't try to go it without God. Don't try to live without Him. It just won't work. Without God there is nothing to live for. With God there is everything to live for. Go with God, the Forgiver, and let go of that old haunted house, filled with the memories of guilt and the ghosts of unhappiness. In Christ God has come for you. In Christ, hurry home where you belong. In Christ God comforts you. Go with God. He has a good word for you: "There is now no condemnation for those who are in Christ Jesus."